What Is Taste?

Jennifer Boothroyd

Lerner Publications

Minneapolis

Lerner Publications Company
A division of Lerner Publishing Group, Inc.
241 First Avenue North
Minneapolis, MN 55401 USA

For reading levels and more information, look up this title at www.lernerbooks.com.

Library of Congress Cataloging-in-Publication Data

    What is taste? / by Jennifer Boothroyd.
       p.   cm. — (Lightning bolt books™—Your amazing senses)
    Includes index.
  ISBN 978–0–7613–4251–9 (lib. bdg. : alk. paper)
  ISBN 978–0–7613–8895–1 (eb pdf)
    1. Taste—Juvenile literature. I. Title.
  QP456.B64 2010
  612.8′7—dc22   2008051847

Manufactured in the United States of America
4–51059–10249–6/3/2021

Contents

Gathering Information

What is your favorite snack?

How does that food
taste? Is it salty?
Is it sweet?

Taste is one of your five senses. You use your tongue to taste things.

Your sense of taste helps you learn about the world. It can also protect you from danger.

The taste—and smell—of milk can warn you if it has gone sour. Sour milk is not safe to drink.

Your Tongue

Your tongue is covered with taste buds. Taste buds are cells that can sense taste.

Your taste buds can sense four basic tastes:

bitter

salty

sour

sweet

Taste buds can sense another taste as well. This taste is called umami. Umami is meaty and flavorful.

Different Tastes:

Bitter

Some things taste bitter—like black licorice.

Or broccoli. Many people dislike bitter foods.

Some kids' taste buds are very sensitive to bitter foods. These kids may not like broccoli.

Salty

Other snacks are salty—like popcorn.

Or potato chips. Eating salty foods can make you thirsty.

Sour

Still other foods are
sour—like crab apples.

Or grapefruit. Your lips may pucker when you taste something sour.

Pucker up! Grapefruit is nutritious, but it is also very sour.

15

Sweet

Many people like sweet foods—
like watermelon.

Or candy.
Watermelon is naturally sweet.
Candy has sugar added to it.

Foods that have sugar added to them are not as healthful as naturally sweet foods.

Umami

Some foods have an umami flavor—like pepperoni.

Or soy sauce. Many Asian foods contain umami.

Soy sauce is made from soybeans. People often use it to flavor rice.

A Matter of Taste

People have different opinions about what tastes good and what does not.

Your brain decides if you think a taste is good or bad.

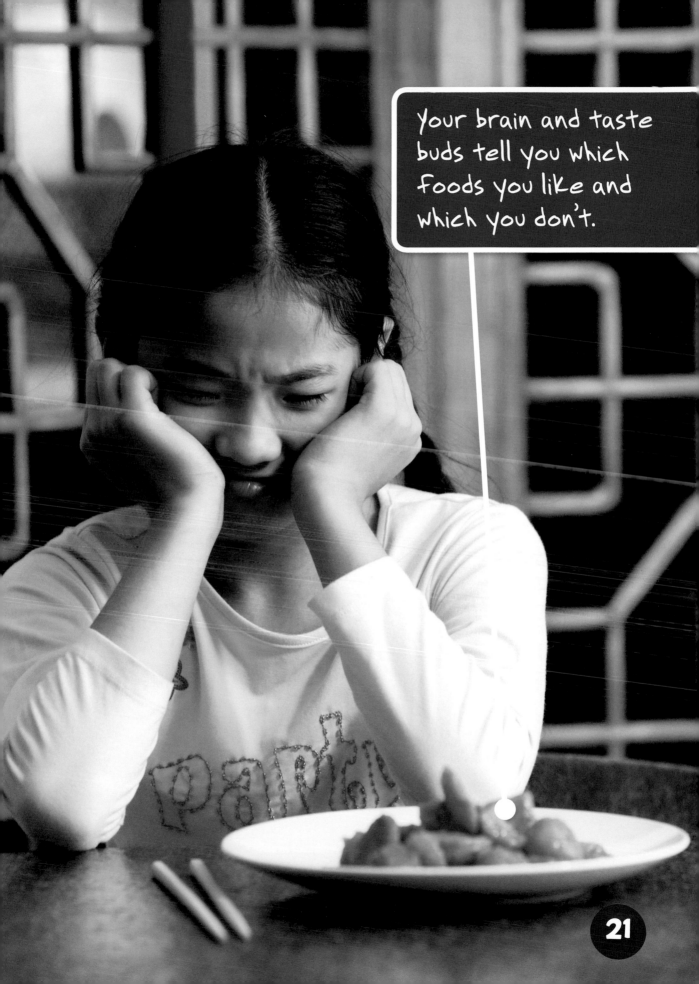

Your brain and taste buds tell you which foods you like and which you don't.

That's why you might think salads taste yummy—

but your friend can't stand them!

Protection from Danger

Our sense of taste can protect us from danger. It stops us from eating things that might make us sick.

WARNING

KEEP AWAY from FEED or FOOD PRODUCTS

POISON

CAUTION—DO NOT DROP

IF LEAKING **DON'T** BREATHE FUMES TOUCH CONTENTS SWALLOW

This is to certify that the contents of this package are properly described by name and are packed and marked and are in proper condition for transportation according to the Regulations prescribed by the Interstate Commerce Commission.

Shipper's name required hereon for shipments by EXPRESS (Printed in U.S.A.) 3-29 774-A

Labels like this warn you not to taste what is inside.

Many poisonous plants and chemicals have a yucky taste.

Hyacinth flowers are poisonous and taste very bad.

People don't like the taste of a rotten apple or moldy bread.

Eating rotten apples can make you sick!

Most people think medicine doesn't taste good. The bad taste stops people from swallowing medicine when they don't need it.

Tasting is an important sense. You use it every day.

Activity
Taste Test

Think about the last time you had to take medicine that tasted bad. Did someone tell you to hold your nose while you took the medicine? Holding your nose can help because your sense of taste is related to your sense of smell. We can't taste foods and medicines very well when we can't smell them. Don't believe this? Ask an adult if you can try this experiment to see how your sense of smell affects your taste.

What you need:
an adult to help you
a utensil for peeling fruits and vegetables
an apple
a raw potato
a pear
a utensil for cutting fruits and vegetables
a cloth to use as a blindfold

What you do:

1. Have the adult peel the apple, the potato, and the pear.

2. Next, have the adult cut the fruits and veggie into similar-sized chunks.

3. Now have the adult tie the cloth around your eyes.

4. Hold your nose, and try taking a bite of each of the foods. See if you can guess which is which.

Once you've made your guesses, think about whether you were able to tell the foods apart. Were you surprised at how hard it was to do? Remember this experiment the next time you have to take some yucky medicine!

Glossary

chemical: a substance used in or produced by chemistry

moldy: a word to describe something that has a fungus called mold growing on it

opinion: the ideas and beliefs that you have about something

poisonous: a word to describe a substance that can kill or harm someone if it is swallowed, inhaled, or sometimes even touched

sense: one of the powers that people and animals use to learn about their surroundings. The five senses are sight, hearing, touch, taste, and smell.

taste bud: a cell that can sense taste

umami: a meaty and flavorful taste. Pepperoni, soy sauce, and many Asian foods have an umami taste.

Further Reading

BBC: Taste
http://www.bbc.co.uk/science/humanbody/body/factfiles/taste/taste_ani_f5.swf

Hewitt, Sally. *Tastes Good!* New York: Crabtree Publishing Company, 2008.

Kids Health: How the Body Works
http://kidshealth.org/kid/htbw

Molter, Carey. *Sense of Taste.* Edina, MN: Abdo, 2001.

Neuroscience for Kids: That's Tasty
http://faculty.washington.edu/chudler/tasty.html

Rotner, Shelley. *Senses on the Farm.* Minneapolis: Millbrook Press, 2009.

Index

Photo Acknowledgments

The images in this book are used with the permission of: © Httin / Dreamstime.com, p. 1; Reflexstock/www.Imagesource.com, pp. 2, 12; © Lisa Pines/Photodisc/Getty Images, p. 4; PhotoAlto Agency RF Collection/Getty Images, p. 5; Reflexstock/Corbis © Royalty-Free/ Corbis, pp. 6, 8, 11; © Brad Wilson/Stone/Getty Images, p. 7; © Araminta/Dreamstime.com, p. 9 (top left); © Dreambigphoto/Dreamstime.com, p. 9 (top right); © Jitkaunv/Dreamstime.com, p. 9 (center left); © Matka/wari/Dreamstime.com, p. 9 (center right); © Sax/Dreamstime.com, p. 9 (bottom left); © Foodfolio Foodfolio/Photolibrary, p. 10; © Paul Burns/Lifesize/Getty Images, p. 13; Reflexstock/Inspirestock/Inspirestock, p. 14; © Martinedegraff/Dreamstime.com, p. 15; © age fotostock/SuperStock, p. 16; © Garry Gay/Photographer's Choice/Getty Images, p. 17; © iStockphoto.com/Juanmonino, p. 18; Reflexstock/Radius © Radius Images, pp. 19, 22 (top); © Mike Kemp/Rubberball Productions/Getty Images, pp. 21, 26; © Todd Strand/Independent Picture Service, pp. 22 (bottom), 29; © Educational Images LTD/Custom Medical Stock Photo, p. 23; © DAJ/Getty Images, p. 24; © Marc Volk/fstop/Getty Images, p. 25; Reflexstock/Stock-broker, p. 27; © Purestock/Photolibrary, p. 30; © Jose Luis Pelaez Inc / Blend Images / Getty Images, p. 31.

Front cover: © Todd Strand/Independent Picture Service (candy and pretzels); © Valerie Potapova/Shutterstock Images (lime); © Betacam-SP/Shutterstock Images (broccoli).